Cryptocurrency Exchanges

Navigating the World of Blockchain-Based Marketplaces

Table of Contents

Chapter 1. Introduction

In this Special Report, "Cryptocurrency Exchanges: Navigating the World of Blockchain-Based Marketplaces," we slice through the seeming complexity of the digital currency world and make it digestible for you. From the origin of cryptocurrencies to their current market dynamics, this report helps to simplify your blockchain journey. It's not about dazzling with terms like 'decentralization' and 'hashing,' rather, it's about breaking down the nuts and bolts of crypto exchanges and their pivotal role in the economy of the future. Grab this report today, and arm yourself with knowledge that demystifies, clarifies, and paves the path towards making informed cryptocurrency decisions. You don't need a degree in computer science to understand crypto exchanges—just a curiosity and this detailed, reader-friendly guide.

Chapter 2. The Birth of Cryptocurrencies: An Introduction

In the late 20th century, with the emergence of the internet, a new frontier was imagined—a world where transactions could be carried out instantly and without intermediaries like banks or governments. The realization of this dream, however, would take another decade. The first step towards this was taken by an anonymous individual or group known as Satoshi Nakamoto.

=== Satoshi Nakamoto and the Concept of Bitcoin

Working under the pseudonym Satoshi Nakamoto, the creator(s) of Bitcoin introduced their vision to the world on Halloween of 2008, in what has come to be known as the Bitcoin White Paper. The White Paper, titled "Bitcoin: A Peer-to-Peer Electronic Cash System," laid the groundwork for what would become the Bitcoin project.

This document proposed a solution to the double-spending problem, a pressing issue in the digital currency world wherein digital assets could potentially be copied and spent more than once. Nakamoto's solution was the introduction of a public ledger system, now known as the blockchain, which would record each transaction and thus prevent issues of duplication.

=== Birth of Blockchain

Blockchain was to be the backbone of Bitcoin, providing a transparent, decentralized, and secure method of recording transactions. It operates as a chain of blocks, each block containing transaction data. Once a block is confirmed by network participants—miners, in the context of Bitcoin—it's added to the blockchain. Altering any data within these blocks is virtually impossible, making the blockchain tamper-proof.

=== Early Bitcoin Transactions and Mining

The first Bitcoin transaction took place on January 12th, 2009, from Satoshi Nakamoto to Hal Finney, a developer and an early cryptocurrency enthusiast. This transaction marked the practical inception of Bitcoin.

Around this time, the practice of Bitcoin mining began. Mining is the process by which new Bitcoins are created and transactions are confirmed and added to the blockchain. Miners compete to solve complex mathematical problems—and the first to solve a problem gets to add a new block to the blockchain and is rewarded with a certain amount of Bitcoins: this number has halved approximately every four years in an event known as the halving.

=== Emergence of Other Cryptocurrencies

While Bitcoin was the first and remains the most popular, it paved the way for other cryptocurrencies, or 'altcoins', some of which were designed to improve upon Bitcoin's perceived limitations. Among the earliest of these was Litecoin, created in 2011 by Charlie Lee, a former Google engineer. Litecoin was touted as the 'silver to Bitcoin's gold'.

Another significant altcoin is Ethereum, which introduced the world to the concept of smart contracts and decentralized applications. Its coin, Ether, is one of the most valuable currencies by market cap after Bitcoin.

=== Introduction of Initial Coin Offerings

A pivotal moment in the growth of the cryptocurrency market was the rise of Initial Coin Offerings (ICOs). An ICO is a form of crowdfunding, where companies raise capital by issuing their own digital tokens in exchange for crypto like Bitcoin or Ether.

While they have been further refined and regulated since, Initial Coin Offerings offered a new way for startup companies to raise funds without seeking traditional methods of venture capital.

=== Cryptocurrencies: A Volatile Investment

From the initial price of less than a cent for a Bitcoin in 2009, to its unprecedented surge to nearly $20,000 in late 2017, then its fall back to around $3,000 in 2018, the path of Bitcoin's value—and by extension, many other cryptocurrencies—has demonstrated extreme volatility. As it stands today, Bitcoin and its peers remain a high-risk, high-reward investment.

=== Today's Cryptocurrency Landscape

Today, there are thousands of cryptocurrencies available, each with their own unique features and uses. Some serve as a digital currency, some provide a platform for building decentralized applications, and some offer a means of privately transferring money around the world.

Regulation initiatives are also increasing around the globe as governments recognize the potential of these digital assets and seek to protect their citizens from potential misuse.

Yes, cryptocurrencies have come a long way from their obscure beginnings. With massive potential for disruption, and despite their volatility, they've already caused substantial ripples throughout the economic landscape. The story of their birth is a testament to the innovation and adaptability characteristic of the digital age. It's also an open-ended tale. Like the internet before it, the world of cryptocurrencies is continually evolving, inviting us all to be part of its ongoing narrative.

Chapter 3. Demystifying Blockchain Technology

Before delving into a comprehensive narrative about blockchain technology, one thing to remember is its fundamental goal—to enable decentralized, transparent, and secure peer-to-peer transactions.

3.1. Understanding the Idea of a Blockchain

A blockchain is a continuously growing list of records, also known as blocks, which are linked and secured using cryptography. Each block typically contains a cryptographic hash of the previous block, a timestamp, and transaction data.

This design makes a blockchain resistant to modification. An individual cannot alter past transactions because all subsequent blocks must also be altered, which requires the collusion of the majority of the network—an essentially impossible task.

Now, how does a blockchain work? It's a simple concept at its core:

1. Transaction Occurs: A party initiates a transaction.

2. Transmission: This transaction is sent out to a network of peer nodes.

3. Block Creation: Each node then adds this transaction to a growing list of other transactions, creating what is called a 'block.'

4. Validation: Blocks are sent to the network, and nodes validate the block and the transactions in it.

5. Chain Addition: Once validated, the block is timestamped and added to an existing chain of other blocks in chronological order.

This process is value-neutral and occurs irrespective of transaction content. So whether it's a currency exchange, a contract execution, or any other form of data transfer, it fundamentally occurs in the same way.

3.2. Structure of a Blockchain

Now let's detail what makes up a 'block' in a blockchain.

Hash: This is a unique series of cryptographic characters that represents specific transaction data. The hash of each block depends on the data it holds, and even a small change will result in a fundamentally different hash. Thus, it is used as a digital fingerprint of the block.

Previous Hash: The identifier for the block that came before. This field links together the "chain" in blockchain, creating an unbroken record of all transactions.

Time Stamp: The time when the block was created. This provides chronological order in the blockchain.

Nonce: This is a number that blockchain miners must find. It, combined with the block content, produces a hash that matches the network's difficulty level.

Transaction Data: The details of the transactions that occurred.

3.3. Decentralization and Transparency

One notable factor about blockchain is its decentralized feature. This means that no single entity has control over the entire network. Rather, it is maintained by a group of nodes, with each node having a complete copy of the entire blockchain.

This decentralization translates into security benefits. Because many nodes hold the blockchain, a would-be attacker cannot alter the transaction history without gaining control of a majority of nodes—an infeasibly difficult feat.

Blockchain's transparency further boosts this security. Every transaction recorded onto a blockchain is visible to all network participants. This public accessibility discourages fraudulent activities.

3.4. The Role of Miners

Miners are vital to blockchain networks. They validate new transactions and record them on the global ledger (blockchain). For this service, they receive a reward in the form of the blockchain's native cryptocurrency (e.g., Bitcoin).

Mining involves solving a mathematical puzzle, which requires computational power. The first miner to find the solution gets to add the new block to the blockchain. This competition ensures that no single miner can control what's included in the blockchain.

3.5. Smart Contracts

An innovation brought about by blockchain technology is smart contracts. These are self-executing contracts where the contract terms are written into code. When the conditions of the contract are met, it executes automatically without the need for a third party.

This brings about many benefits such as speed, accuracy, and security, as the program itself handles the execution, thus eliminating the risks of human errors and reducing the potential for disputes.

3.6. Limitations and Challenges

Despite its potential, blockchain technology still faces several challenges. Its consensus mechanisms like Proof of Work are energy-consuming. There could also be scalability issues, as the speed of transactions in blockchain is slower compared to traditional systems. Moreover, while transparency is usually a benefit, it could also potentially lead to privacy issues.

3.7. The Future of Blockchain Technology

The potential uses for blockchain technology are vast. While it began with cryptocurrency, applications now extend into fields such as supply chain management, voting systems, real estate, healthcare, and more.

In conclusion, understanding blockchain technology doesn't have to seem like an insurmountable task. It takes some getting used to, like any other technology. But once you understand its basic principles—how it operates and the issues it's designed to solve—you will be well equipped to navigate this ever-evolving digital landscape. Make no mistake, blockchain will play an increasingly pivotal role in our future economies and societies. It's not just about cryptocurrencies, it's about a whole new way to transact and interact in the digital world.

Chapter 4. Digging Into Cryptocurrency Exchanges

Cryptocurrency exchanges, colloquially known as crypto exchanges, are at the heart of the digital currency world. They function as the digital marketplaces where traders can exchange cryptocurrencies or digital assets. Crypto exchanges play a vital role, allowing users to buy, sell and trade an array of cryptocurrencies - from the globally recognized Bitcoin and Ethereum to emerging ones like Cardano and Polkadot.

Let's delve deeper into the intriguing world of cryptocurrency exchanges.

4.1. The Birth of Cryptocurrency Exchanges

In the wake of Bitcoin's creation in 2009, a need arose for a marketplace where Bitcoin could be traded for traditional money and other cryptocurrencies. The first crypto exchange, BitcoinMarket.com, sprung up in 2010, initiating trading between Bitcoin and fiat currencies. Not long after, exchanges such as Bitfinex and Binance, capable of handling more diverse trading pairs, paved the way for the complex world of cryptocurrency exchanges today.

4.2. Functioning of a Cryptocurrency Exchange

Almost all crypto exchanges start with a user creating an account. Once the account is verified, the user can deposit fiat currency, some form of digital currency, or both into their exchange wallet.

From here, the user navigates to the trading interface, which displays a list of possible cryptocurrency trading pairs. The user can then specify the amount and price at which they wish to buy or sell and execute the order. The exchange then matches this order with a corresponding one from another user and completes the transaction.

Importantly, the exchange doesn't directly sell or buy currencies. Its chief role is to provide a platform that connects buyers and sellers.

4.3. Centralized Versus Decentralized Exchanges

Two main types of crypto exchanges predominate in the market: centralized exchanges (CEXs) and decentralized exchanges (DEXs).

CEXs function similarly to traditional banks. They act as trusted third parties that facilitate transactions between participants. While this centralization brings advantages like quick trades and user-friendly interfaces, it also leads to security risks, as CEXs are attractive targets for hackers.

On the contrary, DEXs allow peer-to-peer transactions, eliminating the need for intermediaries. Users control their funds and carry out transactions directly in their wallets. DEXs offer enhanced privacy and control; however, they also pose their users risk since losses due to scams or user errors are prevalent.

4.4. Understanding Trading Options

Crypto exchanges offer various types of trades, from simple to complex. The most frequent are:

1. Market Order: This signifies a trade at the current market price.
2. Limit Order: It involves setting a specific or better price for the

trade.

3. Stop Order: This order becomes active only after a defined price level is reached.

For more sophisticated traders, exchanges offer 'Futures trading' and 'Margin trading'.

4.5. Threading Security Threads

Security stands crucial in the sphere of cryptocurrency exchanges. The decentralized nature and digital aspect of cryptocurrencies make them attractive targets for cybercriminals. Nonetheless, exchanges adopt various strategies to mitigate these threats. These include two-factor authentication (2FA), end-to-end encryption, cold storage, and employing secure protocols.

4.6. Regulatory Aspects

Crypto exchanges vary globally based on regional regulatory standards. Some countries have clear regulations, while others work in legal gray areas, and a few have banned cryptocurrencies. Understanding the regulations for crypto exchanges in your region is crucial before participating in trading.

4.7. The Role of Cryptocurrency Exchanges in the Crypto Economy

Cryptocurrency exchanges are the economic engines driving the blockchain revolution. They enable fundraising for projects via Initial Coin Offerings (ICOs), provide price discovery mechanisms, and make cryptocurrencies accessible to the mass.

4.8. Choices Galore

Today's crypto landscape boasts a broad spectrum of exchanges offering a variety of services. For novice traders, there are straightforward platforms like Coinbase. For those seeking advanced trading features, exchanges like Binance offer a wide range of tools and assets.

Choosing an exchange depends on several factors: the user's location, preferred cryptocurrencies, user interface preference, and desired security level.

This chapter aimed to give a comprehensive understanding of what takes to use cryptocurrency exchanges. However, remember, while the world of cryptocurrency offers immense potential, it also comes with its set of risks. Take informed decisions, keep abreast of the often volatile market trends, and proceed wisely in this complex yet exhilarating world of digital currency.

In the chapters to follow, we'll delve into the more intricate elements of blockchain technology, trading strategies, and the future of crypto exchanges. Until then, happy trading!

Chapter 5. Key Players: Highlighting Major Cryptocurrency Exchanges

Consider the world of cryptocurrency exchanges as a bustling, global marketplace. While the underlying technology of cryptographic blockchains and peer-to-peer networks diligently secure every transaction, the accessibility of these digital currencies and the ease of their exchange is coded by an intricate web of platforms collectively dubbed 'crypto exchanges'. Each exchange comes with its own unique features, dynamics, and operational idiosyncrasies, but they all contribute to a singular mission - to connect buyers and sellers in the nascent, powerful world of blockchain-backed finance.

5.1. Coinbase

Ebbs of the global capital market find a reflection in San Francisco-based Coinbase. Launched in 2012, Coinbase's appeal lies in its simplicity, robust security measures, and wide array of available digital assets. As of 2021, Coinbase boasts over 56 million users, managing more than $223 billion in digital assets.

Focusing on creating an accessible crypto marketplace, Coinbase supports a multitude of cryptocurrencies beyond Bitcoin, including Ethereum, Ripple, and Litecoin. Equipped with a user-friendly interface, the platform allows its users to buy, sell, and store crypto, becoming a convenient 'one-stop-shop' for novices.

Despite the widely praised user experience, some users have noted the platform's higher fees compared to other exchanges. Yet, ease of use, a broad scope of resources, and high liquidity make Coinbase essentially unavoidable when charting the landscape of major cryptocurrency exchanges.

5.2. Binance

Born amidst the 2017 cryptocurrency boom, Binance has demonstrated an extensive flourish in the last few years. Headquartered in Malta, Binance allows users to trade more than 150 different cryptocurrencies. Known for its low fees and impressive liquidity, Binance affirms itself as a cutting-edge exchange, offering advanced trading features like futures and options.

Prominently, Binance introduced its native Binance Coin (BNB) that not only works as a transactional token within the platform but also offers a transaction fee discount to its holders. Notably, Binance's earlier migration to a more robust blockchain, the Binance Smart Chain, has indeed strengthened its reputation among the industry's more technically proficient communities.

However, the company has faced regulatory scrutiny worldwide, questioning its opaque operations. In spite of regulatory challenges and potential vulnerabilities, Binance stands tall in the crypto exchanges landscape.

5.3. Kraken

Founded in 2011, San Francisco-based Kraken has endured multiple crypto cycles, gaining trust and users along the way. Offering an extensive range of cryptocurrencies for trading, Kraken not only supports common fiat currencies like the US dollar and Euro but also niche offerings like the Canadian dollar and the Japanese yen.

Kraken sets itself apart with advanced features like margin trading and futures. Especially for the more seasoned traders hunting for volatility, Kraken presents a competent platform. Moreover, the platform has one of the cleanest security records in the industry, shored by features like two-factor authentication and cold storage for digital assets.

The main critique of Kraken tends to circle around its less user-friendly interface, somewhat limiting its appeal to beginners. Yet for seasoned traders looking for an exhaustive range of cryptocurrencies, fiat pairs, and trading features, Kraken pitches a strong case.

5.4. Gemini

Born out of the USA's regulatory stronghold, New York-based Gemini has earned its reputation as one of the most compliant and secure cryptocurrency exchanges worldwide. Founded in 2014 by the Winklevoss twins, the platform is fully licensed and regulated, giving it a higher level of credibility than most of its counterparts.

Gemini stands out with its robust security measures, including FDIC insurance on USD deposits, and all digital assets are held in a trust on customer's behalf. The platform offers a modest selection of cryptocurrencies for trade compared with the wider market but excels in compliance, security, and reliability.

Gemini's primary criticism is its relatively high fees compared to other exchanges. Nonetheless, for those willing to trade cost for security and peace of mind, Gemini stands as a formidable choice.

In this rapidly evolving landscape, no single platform can claim to perfectly serve every trader's preferences. These major players can guide you in understanding the variegated features and operational frameworks at play in the world of cryptocurrency exchanges.

Chapter 6. The Art of Trading Cryptocurrencies

The notion of trading fiats - the traditional currencies we use in our daily life - is quite known to us all. It's no different when it comes to cryptocurrencies. The nature may be digital rather than physical, but the principles remain the same. Let's dive into the art of trading cryptocurrencies.

6.1. Understanding the Cryptocurrency Market

Before you start trading, it's fundamental to understand the cryptocurrency market dynamics. This domain differs from traditional finance and stock markets in several ways. Its 24/7 open market, high volatility, and global market access make it unique. Being digital, they are unbound by geography or traditional market hours. Volatility, while daunting for the unprepared, also harbors potential for high return on investments, albeit at increased risk.

6.2. Identifying Cryptocurrency Types

Broadly, cryptocurrencies can be classified into Bitcoin and Altcoins. Bitcoin, being the first, stands in a league of its own. Altcoins or 'alternative coins' are the other coins launched following Bitcoin's success. Ethereum, Ripple, Litecoin are a few popular names among a sea of altcoins. Each cryptocurrency bears its own purpose, technology, and market. Trading strategies will differ based on these variables.

6.3. Choosing a Reliable Cryptocurrency Exchange

A cryptocurrency exchange is a virtual platform where you can buy, sell or trade cryptocurrencies. Some popular exchanges include Binance, Coinbase, and Bitfinex. When choosing an exchange, consider factors such as security, user interface, trading fees, coin availability, and customer support.

6.4. Comprehending Trading Pairs

In a cryptocurrency exchange, the value of a coin is determined in relation to another coin or a fiat. This is known as a trading pair. It is critical to understand how pairs work as this forms the basis of trading. Usually, you will find pairs like BTC/USD, ETH/BTC, etc. In this case, the first currency is the "base," and the second is the "quote" currency.

6.5. Applying Technical Analysis and Chart Patterns

A trader's universal tools are chart patterns and technical analysis. Understanding these can drastically help make informed trading decisions. Chart patterns signal potential trends or reversals in price. It's like reading the market's behaviour graphically. Common patterns include 'Head and Shoulders,' 'Double Top/Bottom,' and 'Cup and Handle.'

Technical analysis, on the other hand, utilizes indicators and statistical analysis to predict future price movements. Popular indicators used are Moving Averages (MA), Relative Strength Index (RSI), and Moving Average Convergence Divergence (MACD).

6.6. Planning the Trade and Execution

Once acquainted with the basics, the next step is to plan your trade. This includes setting objectives, creating a risk management strategy, defining entry and exit points and specifying stop loss and take profit levels. A trader's best companion is discipline to stick to the plan despite market fluctuations. Finally, place the trade on the exchange and monitor it closely according to your plan.

6.7. Mastering the Emotional Game

Last but certainly not least is managing your emotions. Greed and fear can often lead to irrational decisions, harming potential profits. The key here is to be patient, stay disciplined, and follow the plan you put in place.

Cryptocurrency trading is a complex and intricate skill that requires patience, diligence, and unbroken learning. The high volatility nature of this market does house potential for high returns but carries significant risk. It's therefore important to approach this world with an informed strategy, constant analysis, and emotional control. Written with clarity and simplicity, this guide aims to navigate you smoothly into the world of crypto trading. Master this art, and you might just be on your way to becoming a successful cryptocurrency trader. Sticking to these guidelines will put you in a strong and informed position to seize the myriad opportunities this sector has to offer.

Chapter 7. Security Measures: A Deep Dive into Crypto Exchange Protections

Despite its groundbreaking innovations, the world of cryptocurrencies has remained a constant theatre for scam artists, hackers, and security breaches. Exchanges exposed to cyber threats have put billions of dollars at stake, causing a ripple of doubt among potential investors and users. As such, ensuring security in crypto exchanges has involved a myriad of safety measures, advanced technological applications, and stringent regulations.

7.1. Understanding the Nature of Cyber Threats in Crypto Exchanges

Cyber threats in crypto exchanges are diverse and complex, ranging from instances of phishing to outright system infiltration. These threats pose significant financial risks to both the exchange operators and their users. In phishing attacks, ill-intentioned individuals trick users into divulging their sensitive information, such as passwords and private keys, exposing their wallets to theft. System infiltration is where hackers breach the exchange's system, potentially causing substantial financial losses, like in the infamous Mt. Gox incident where over 740,000 Bitcoins were lost.

Furthermore, Distributed Denial of Service (DDoS) attacks overload an exchange's system, rendering it dysfunctional and preventing users from accessing their accounts. These attacks not only disrupt the smooth functioning of the exchange but also create trading discrepancies, exposing the exchange and its users to potential financial risk.

7.2. Implementing Fundamental Security Measures

For the effective protection of both user assets and the credibility of the exchange, certain fundamental security measures need to be implemented. These include two-factor authentication (2FA), cold storage of assets, and encryption.

2FA provides an additional layer of defense beyond a username and password combination. In most cases, enabling 2FA would mean receiving a unique code every time a user logs in to their account, adding another checkpoint for unauthorized users.

Cold storage involves transferring assets from an internet-connected computer (hot storage) to an offline environment. It ensures the majority of user assets cannot be accessed remotely by would-be criminals.

Data encryption is another critical practice in crypto exchanges. From user account details to transaction information, every bit of data is encrypted using advanced concepts such as hash functions and cryptography keys to ensure security.

7.3. Advanced Security Applications

Beyond the fundamental measures, crypto exchanges also harness more advanced forms of protection. For one, the deployment of Machine Learning (ML) algorithms has been instrumental in identifying suspicious activities and mitigating cyber threats. These algorithms analyze a vast range of data points and predict abnormal patterns, providing an additional layer of security.

Some crypto exchanges also employ the use of biometric security measures. While these technologies are somewhat still in their embryonic stage, future systems may even use face recognition or fingerprint scanning to ensure the account holder is the one accessing their assets.

7.4. Regulatory Compliance

Compliance with regulations is also integral to the security of crypto exchanges. While the regulation of cryptocurrencies remains a hot topic globally, several jurisdictions have taken steps to lay down rules for crypto exchanges, which not only legitimizes their operations but provides an additional layer of security.

Whether it's abiding by Know Your Customer (KYC) requirements or adhering to Anti-Money Laundering (AML) guidelines, crypto exchanges have a duty to adhere strictly to all relevant regulations. Non-compliance risks severe reputational damage, financial penalties, and can potentially result in shutting down the exchange.

7.5. Continuous Vigilance: The Pathway to Peace of Mind

Efficient digital security measures require constant vigilance. Remember, even with the strongest security measures in place, no system is entirely impervious to risks. As cyber threats continue to evolve, so must the defenses of crypto exchanges. Continuous re-evaluation and upgrading of safety measures are thus paramount.

7.6. Conclusion

Crypto exchanges have become the linchpin of the digital currency ecosystem. Ensuring their security is not a destination but a continuous journey, always adapting and improving in stride with the ever-evolving cyber threats. As such, understanding the security measures and processes in place is essential for anyone getting involved in the crypto space. Stay knowledgeable, stay secure!

Chapter 8. Regulatory Landscapes: Understanding the Legalities

Introduction to Regulatory Landscapes

Regulation in the cryptocurrency industry is unique, given the relatively recent emergence alongside the often borderless nature of digital currencies. While cryptocurrencies and digital asset exchanges are subject to a variety of laws across different jurisdictions, they're also an area of interest for lawmakers, who must balance innovation, investor protection, and financial stability.

8.1. Know your Jurisdictions

The first thing to bear in mind when dealing with crypto exchanges and the legal landscape is that every jurisdiction has different laws and regulations. Some regions are more friendly towards cryptocurrencies, others extremely cautious.

The US, for example, operates under a state-level licensing regime, with cryptocurrencies classified as commodities, securities, or money, depending on their individual characteristics and use cases. However, in the European Union, cryptocurrencies aren't classified as legal tender, but operators providing crypto services are required to follow anti-money laundering (AML) and counter-terrorism financing (CTF) regulations.

In Asia, the regulatory environment is varied. China once wholly banned cryptocurrencies, while Singapore and Japan have sought to establish regulated, but cryptocurrency-friendly, financial ecosystems.

8.2. The Regulatory Bodies and Crypto Laws

Various regulatory bodies have jurisdiction over cryptocurrency exchanges, each with their own specific remit and powers. In the US, this includes the Securities and Exchange Commission (SEC), the Commodity Futures Trading Commission (CFTC), and the Financial Crimes Enforcement Network (FinCEN).

These organizations all maintain their own sets of rules and guidelines for cryptocurrency exchanges. The SEC, for example, follows the landmark "Howey Test" to ascertain whether a cryptocurrency constitutes a security, which impacts its degree of regulatory oversight.

AML and CTF laws are also widespread in the crypto industry. Often, exchanges must implement systems and controls to prevent, detect, and report on potential instances of money laundering or terrorist financing. This generally involves "know your customer" (KYC) principles which require exchanges to collect and verify identity information from their users.

8.3. Registration Process for Cryptocurrency Exchanges

Registration is an important part of running a legitimate cryptocurrency exchange. Procedures vary by jurisdiction, but often include submitting applications, paying licensing fees, and demonstrating compliance with relevant regulations.

For example, in the US, if a crypto exchange's business falls under FinCEN's jurisdiction, the exchange must register as a money services business, implement an AML program, and keep robust records, among other requirements.

8.4. Dealing with Regulation Changes

As the crypto industry evolves and matures, so does its regulatory landscape. Laws and guidelines often change, sometimes radically, necessitating exchanges to adapt continually. Keeping up to date with regulatory changes in multiple jurisdictions is an ongoing challenge for these businesses.

8.5. Self-Regulation in the Crypto Industry

While formal regulatory places an essential role in the cryptocurrency landscape, self-regulation plays its part too. Several industry bodies and associations have formed, promoting a high standard of ethics and professionalism within the crypto market. These self-regulatory bodies often work along with regulators, giving them important insights into the industry's intricacies.

8.6. The Future of Cryptocurrency Regulation

While we can't predict the future with certainty, it's clear that regulatory bodies across the world are taking increased interest in digital assets, and this trend is expected to continue. Cryptocurrencies are likely to face more stringent regulation as the sector matures and becomes more mainstream.

As with any investment, understanding the regulatory landscape of cryptocurrencies is vital. It can help not only in making informed investment decisions, but it also aids in determining the future direction of the market and anticipating potential shifts or risks.

In conclusion, navigating the regulatory landscape of crypto exchanges can be complex, but it is essential for both investors and platform operators. Regulations are designed to protect consumers, prevent illegal activity, and maintain financial stability. As cryptocurrencies become more mainstream, it's likely that the regulatory environment will tighten further, making it even more important for investors and traders to understand the legal intricacies of this exciting space.

Chapter 9. Investment Strategies for Crypto Exchange Markets

Investing in cryptocurrency exchange markets can be both enticing and challenging, due to its significant potential for returns and its inherent volatility. This chapter will explore detailed investment strategies to navigate this dynamic market.

9.1. Building a Balanced Crypto Portfolio

One of the core strategies for investing in crypto exchange markets is to build a balanced portfolio. This involves crafting a range of cryptos that covers various sectors or types within the crypto landscape, from major coins like Bitcoin (BTC) and Ethereum (ETH) to promising novices and altcoins. This approach spreads the risk across multiple assets and can help you weather market volatility.

There are numerous strategies to build a balanced portfolio, such as:

- *Sector-based Strategy*: This approach involves investing in cryptos based on their use-case sectors like fintech, healthcare, logistics, entertainment, etc. Each sector represents potential growth paths that could result in significant returns.

- *Risk-level Based Strategy*: This involves dividing your portfolio based on the risk associated with each crypto. High-risk crypto (often newer or less well-known coins) might have higher return potential but also a higher chance of loss. Balanced with low-risk assets (such as BTC or ETH), this approach can help manage the overall risk level.

- *Market Cap Based Strategy*: In this approach, the allocation of assets is based on the market cap of each crypto. Investors may allocate a higher percentage to cryptos with higher market caps and vice versa. This strategy can also aid in risk mitigation.

9.2. Crypto-Centric versus Diversification

While a balanced crypto portfolio is a good starting point, another strategy to consider is diversification beyond just cryptocurrencies. Spreading your investment across different asset classes (like stocks, bonds, commodities, real estate) can help balance the inherently volatile nature of cryptos.

Diversification can either be:

- *Asset Level*: Where you divide your assets across different investment classes.

- *Geographical Level*: Where you invest across different geographical markets worldwide.

It's important to remember that even within the crypto market, diversity is key. Investing all your money in a single project or sector can increase the risk exponent.

9.3. Technical Analysis for Crypto Investments

Technical analysis (TA) is a common technique used by investors and traders which involves predicting the future price movements of cryptocurrencies based on their historical data. TA employs a myriad of indicators and chart patterns to identify potential trends or reversal points in the market.

Key technical analysis indicators in crypto trading can include:

- *Moving Averages*: Useful for identifying trends over a specific time period.

- *Relative Strength Index (RSI)*: It shows overbought or oversold conditions in the market.

- *Bollinger Bands*: These provide a relative definition of high and low price levels at a glance.

- *Volume*: An indicator of the interest level in a particular coin at a specific price level.

While TA can't predict future prices with 100% accuracy, it can help investors make more informed decisions on when to buy, hold, or sell a particular crypto.

9.4. Fundamental Analysis of Crypto Projects

Fundamental analysis is about evaluating a crypto project based on its fundamentals—the technology it runs on (like the blockchain tech and its specific features), project use case, tokenomics, team behind the project, and more.

Some of the key elements for fundamental analysis include:

- *Project Whitepapers*: This offers insights on the project's technical details, its purpose, and a roadmap of its future developments.

- *Project Development Activity*: Regular updates and activity on the project's GitHub page can indicate a committed team working on the project.

- *Partnerships and Alliances*: Brands or companies partnering with a crypto project can be a positive sign of credibility.

- *Community Support*: A highly engaged community indicates

robust support for a crypto project.

With these investment strategies wrapped under your belt, it's crucial to stay abreast with the rapidly changing landscape in crypto exchange markets and adjust your strategies accordingly. Apart from that, keep emotions at bay while navigating through bull runs or bear markets, and focus on long-term gains.

Remember that owning and controlling your investment decisions, irrespective of market buzz or hype and making informed decisions based on detailed analysis are vital to stay ahead in the crypto market.

Chapter 10. Future Prospects: Trends and Predictions

When we anticipate the future of cryptocurrencies and their exchanges, we need to consider technological advancements, policy changes, market demands, and idiosyncrasies in global economic structures. A few trends and patterns stand out as particularly plausible, given today's landscape.

10.1. The Mainstreaming of Cryptocurrencies

The last decade has marked cryptocurrencies transition, from being confined to small circles of early adopters to attracting the attention of large financial institutions and governments. Cryptocurrencies are increasingly gaining prominence in mainstream finance due to their unique advantages—anonymity, speed, cost savings on transactions, and exclusion of intermediaries.

Recent developments in corporate adoption signal this shift. Companies like Tesla, Square, and MicroStrategy have started adding Bitcoin to their balance sheets. Payment companies like PayPal and Visa are incorporating crypto in their offerings. Beyond corporates, Central Banks worldwide are exploring digital currencies (CBDCs), an acknowledgement that digitization of money is inevitable.

10.2. Regulatory Measures and Cryptocurrencies

Given cryptocurrencies' scale and impact, regulatory trends will significantly influence their future. Currently, there's a wide variance in regulatory approaches—some countries have embraced cryptocurrencies, others have outright banned them. The evolving legislative landscape indicates a move towards comprehensive regulation, which involves protecting consumers, ensuring financial stability, and preventing criminal activities.

Transition to regulation may bring certain challenges initially such as market volatility and investor speculation, but in the long term, it is expected to lend credibility, ensuring sustainable growth and wider adoption.

10.3. The Evolution of Decentralized Exchanges

Decentralized Exchanges (DEXs) are among the most notable developments within the crypto sphere. DEXs operate without an intermediary, making transactions more transparent and reducing the risk of hacks. Current trends suggest that improvements in the efficiency, speed, and reliability of DEXs could lead to their greater market share.

However, DEXs will have to address the twin challenges of scalability and user experience to compete with centralized exchanges. Centralized exchanges offer faster trade execution, easier-to-use interfaces, and customer support, giving them an edge over their decentralized counterparts.

10.4. The Role of Stablecoins in the Cryptocurrency Market

Stablecoins, cryptocurrencies pegged to a stable asset like gold or USD, provide transactional stability while maintaining the cryptocurrency benefits. As a bridge between the worlds of traditional finance and crypto, stablecoins are expected to play an increasingly significant role.

As more businesses accept cryptocurrencies, stablecoins could reduce market volatility, making them an attractive proposition. Further, stablecoins could also be an entry point for institutional investment, driving crypto adoption.

10.5. Integration of Financial Services with Cryptocurrencies

The integration of cryptocurrency with traditional financial services is another trend that's likely to accelerate in the future. Already, we're witnessing a rise in crypto-specific financial products and services—crypto loans, insurance, savings accounts, and even retirement funds.

Such integration can help cryptocurrencies gain legitimacy, encourage mainstream adoption, and increase the market's overall liquidity. As a result, crypto-based financial products are expected to proliferate over the coming years.

10.6. Investments and Institutional Adoption

Increased institutional investment is another trend to keep an eye on. Traditionally, institutional investors have been wary of cryptocurrencies due to their high volatility and perceived risk. But with improved regulatory clarity, we can expect more institutional players to enter the crypto space.

This could also fuel innovation in crypto exchanges by promoting sophisticated financial instruments like futures, options, and ETFs. Furthermore, institutional adoption could lead to better price discovery and reduced volatility in the crypto market.

There's never been an era of finance as transformative as the one we're in now. Through harnessing the potential of cryptocurrencies and preparing for the challenges they bring, exchanges stand to play a vital role in shaping the economy of the future. The proliferation of DEXs, growing regulatory oversight, the rise of stablecoins, and integration with traditional financial products—all these trends are redefining what's conceivable in our financial system. How these possibilities unfold largely hinges on our collective choices in navigating this complex terrain.

Chapter 11. A Practical Guide: How to Start Trading on Crypto Exchanges

Trading on a crypto exchange may seem like a daunting task, but even novice users can navigate this process effectively with proper guidance. This guide aims to provide a detailed, step-by-step approach to getting started with crypto exchanges.

11.1. Understand What Cryptocurrency is

To trade cryptocurrencies successfully, you first need to understand what they are. Cryptocurrencies are digital or virtual currencies that use cryptography for security, making them nearly impossible to counterfeit or double spend. Famously decentralized, they operate on technology known as blockchains, which are decentralized ledgers of all transactions across a peer-to-peer network. The most well-known cryptocurrency is Bitcoin (BTC), though many other variants (called altcoins) exist, including Ethereum (ETH), Ripple (XRP), and Litecoin (LTC).

11.2. Choose the Right Cryptocurrency Exchange

There are hundreds of crypto exchanges available, each offering different features. Here are a few aspects to consider while choosing:

- **Security**: Consider two-factor authentication (2FA), withdrawal whitelists, and other security features. Look for an exchange with a good track record— one that hasn't suffered significant hacks in the past.

- **Regulation**: Regulated exchanges are subject to controls and audits, providing additional protection for users. Consider where the exchange is regulated and by which authority.

- **Liquidity**: An exchange with high liquidity can process large volumes of trades and offers tighter spreads. Check the exchange's daily trading volumes.

- **Trading pairs**: Not all exchanges support all cryptocurrencies. Check if your preferred coins are traded on the exchange you are considering.

- **User interface**: Choose an exchange with a clear and easy-to-use interface, particularly if you're a beginner.

- **Fees**: Exchanges charge fees on trades. These can add up, particularly with high volumes of trading, so make sure you understand the charges.

11.3. Setting Up an Account

Once you've chosen an exchange, you'll need to set up an account. This process usually involves providing some personal information due to Know Your Customer (KYC) regulations. You may also need to provide a form of ID and likely set up 2FA for added security.

11.4. Learn to Navigate the Exchange

Familiarize yourself with the chosen exchange's platform. Most will have a 'dashboard' or 'home' page displaying a variety of information including current prices, market trends, recent trades, and your account balance. Make sure you understand how to conduct a trade, view your transaction history, deposit and withdraw funds, and implement stop-loss orders.

11.5. Make a Deposit

The next step is to deposit funds. This involves transferring cryptocurrency from a wallet (either a software wallet on your computer or a hardware wallet) to your trading account, or depositing fiat currency using a bank transfer or credit card.

11.6. Place Your First Trade

Now you're ready to make a trade. Typically, this involves:

1. Selecting a trading pair (the two currencies you'll be trading)

2. Choosing a type of order (e.g., a market order, which buys at the current market price, or a limit order, which only buys at a certain price or better)

3. Confirming the details of the order

4. Executing the trade

Check, double-check, and triple-check all details before pressing 'confirm.' Mistakes can prove costly in trading!

11.7. Understand Trading Strategies

Familiarize yourself with different trading strategies, like day trading (making trades within the daily price movement), swing trading (holding trades over a period of days or weeks), and holding (buying and holding a cryptocurrency in anticipation of long-term price appreciation).

11.8. Keep Tabs on Market News and Developments

Stay informed about market trends. Many exchanges provide news feeds and analysis tools. Regularly reading up on cryptocurrency market trends and news will help you make informed decisions.

11.9. Be Aware of Regulations and Taxes

Finally, be aware of pertinent regulations and tax obligations in your country of residence. In the wake of cryptocurrency's rising popularity, many countries have developed regulations for digital currencies. Familiarize yourself with these rules to ensure compliance.

In conclusion, while the world of crypto exchanges may seem overwhelming at first, with careful study and caution, you can navigate it successfully. Always remember: while the potential rewards can be significant, so too are the risks. Aim to be an informed and cautious trader, and you could make your mark in the vibrant world of crypto trading.